Let the River Run Silver Again!

How One School Helped Return the American Shad
to the Potomac River – And How You Too Can
Help Protect and Restore Our Living Waters

Sandy Burk

The McDonald & Woodward Publishing Company
Blacksburg, Virginia

LET THE RIVER RUN SILVER AGAIN!: HOW ONE SCHOOL HELPED RETURN THE AMERICAN SHAD TO THE POTOMAC RIVER – AND HOW YOU TOO CAN HELP PROTECT AND RESTORE OUR LIVING WATERS

The McDonald & Woodward Publishing Company
Blacksburg, Virginia, and Granville, Ohio

All rights reserved. First printing May 2005; second printing February 2007
Printed in Canada by Friesens, Altona, Manitoba

15 14 13 12 11 10 09 08 07   10 9 8 7 6 5 4 3 2

Library of Congress Cataloging-in-Publication Data

Burk, Sandy, 1962-
  Let the river run silver again! : how one school helped return the American shad to the Potomac River--and how you too can help protect and restore our living waters / Sandy Burk.
     p. cm.
  ISBN 0-939923-95-5 (pbk. : alk. paper)
  1. American shad--Reintroduction--Potomac River--Citizen participation. 2. Westbrook Elementary School (Bethesda, Md.)--Students. 3. Watershed restoration--Maryland--Little Falls Branch Watershed--Citizen participation. I. Title.
  QL638.C64B87 2005
  639.9'7745--dc22

                                                                                   2005009218

FIGURE CREDITS: Anacostia Watershed Society – 33 (logo); Mike Bailey – 25 (top); Andrea Barnes – 25 (bottom); Jamie Baxter – back cover (second from top); Robert Burk – 13 (right); Sandy Burk – back cover (third and fifth from top), 14, 15 (middle and bottom), 18 (top), 28, 34; Chesapeake Bay Foundation – 24 (bottom), 33 (logo); Jim Cummins / Interstate Commission on the Potomac River Basin – front cover inset, back cover (top), 8 (top), 32; Curtis Dalpra / Interstate Commission on the Potomac River Basin – 12, 15 (top), 18 (bottom), 29; Jen Dotson / Interstate Commission on the Potomac River Basin – 8 (bottom), 33 (logo); Environmental Concern – 20; Charles Gale – 27 (top); Sandi Geddes – back cover (fourth from top), 4, 13 (bottom), 16, 19; David Hawxhurst, *www.hawkshurst.com* – 21 (top and bottom); Izaak Walton League of America – 33 (logo); Living Classrooms – 33 (logo); McDonald & Woodward Publishing Company – 6; Steve Minkkinen / US Fish and Wildlife Service – 27 (all except top); Mount Vernon Ladies' Association – 10; National Park Service – 33 (top); *Potomac Almanac* – 11; Robert Robbins – 26; Steve Saari – 22; Joann Symons – 24 (top); The Potomac Conservancy – 33 (logo); US Army Corps of Engineers – 23 (left); US Fish and Wildlife Service – 7 (modified), 9, 35; US Fish and Wildlife Service / Harrison Lake National Fish Hatchery – 17 (right); *Washington Post* – 23 (right); John Page Williams – 31. The image of the American shad that is used throughout the book was provided by the US Fish and Wildlife Service.

FRONT COVER INSET PHOTOGRAPH: Students from Westbrook Elementary School making their initial release of American Shad into the Potomac River in 1996. The young fish being released by these students had been raised in their classroom from eggs collected earlier in the year.

Table of Contents

Preface

Armed with nets, microscopes, and new knowledge from modern science, communities, schools, and individuals have joined the challenge to clean up our waters and help bring back their aquatic life.

In 1995, along the banks of the Potomac River in Bethesda, Maryland, Westbrook Elementary School and its community joined other schools and conservation organizations in the area to help clean up Little Falls stream and to

Each year, student members of Westbrook school's Aqua Eagles Ecology Club monitored Little Falls stream.

help restore populations of a once plentiful but now threatened fish, the historically important American shad, to the Potomac River. The determined and enthusiastic efforts of students and others in their community were vital parts of this comprehensive program to improve the environmental quality of their local waters and their watershed. *Let the River Run Silver Again!* tells the story of Westbrook school's contribution to this successful undertaking, and in doing so presents a model of environmental restoration that can be carried out with similar programs wherever living waters are to be found.

The greater part of this book describes Westbrook school's success story — the story of how one elementary school was inspired to take on this project that spanned several years of the students' education and exposed them to the processes of community cooperation; the workings of government; scientific procedures; shared success; and considerations in making career choices. This part of the book chronicles the events to which the students can relate, and an epilogue summarizes the successes of the project.

Sidebars provide supplementary information for some important concepts that are introduced in this section, and a glossary provides definitions of technical terms that have been used in the Westbrook success story.

The remaining part of the book provides questions and information useful in devising waterway and watershed projects in other areas. A page of questions is provided for readers who might wish to reflect upon or discuss some fundamental insights revealed by the Westbrook — or any other similar — project. Generalized steps for creating a successful water-related project are listed, and these are followed by names of agencies and organizations that can be helpful in suggesting, defining, and helping to implement such projects.

Teachers, students, home schoolers, nature center staffs, community groups, ecology clubs, youth groups, and other individuals and organizations are encouraged to use this book for inspiration, information, and planning when developing or working on projects to help revitalize or restore their waters and watersheds.

Acknowledgments

I gratefully acknowledge the teachers and students of Westbrook Elementary School for sharing their experiences with me for use in this book. The dialogue presented here is based on my interviews and recordings of Westbrook Elementary School students and teachers and professional members of the shad program staff. Special thanks are due to Westbrook teachers Sandi Geddes, Beth Schmelzer, and Nancy Wong for their extraordinary help in providing very helpful information and many of the photographs that I have used in this book.

For the invaluable contributions of time, talent, and knowledge that have greatly enhanced the quality of this book, I extend special thanks to John Page Williams and Jennifer Cassou of the Chesapeake Bay Foundation, Jim Cummins and Curtis Dalpra of the Interstate Commission on the Potomac River Basin, and Robert Burk, my father.

I also would like to recognize the Chesapeake Bay Trust for providing generous financial support to the Schools in Schools program.

Sandy Burk, April 2005

Never doubt that a small group of thoughtful, committed citizens can change the world. Indeed, it's the only thing that ever has.

Margaret Meade

The Mighty Journey of an Important Fish

American shad, the largest member of the herring family, is a type of *anadromous* fish — fish that spend part of their lives in the ocean and part of their lives in bays and rivers. While in the ocean, American shad eat plankton and, in turn, are eaten by larger animals such as bottle-nosed dolphins.

Each spring, however, millions of silvery adult American shad travel hundreds or thousands of miles from the

Atlantic and Pacific oceans to return to the freshwater rivers of the United States and Canada where they were born. Here they will find suitable sites, spawn, and then return to the sea. From the eggs they lay and fertilize will come the next generation of young shad.

The return of the shad each year to the waters of their birth is a critical part of the life cycle of the species and of the ecology of many of our bays and rivers. These annual runs of American shad were an important source of food for many species of fish and birds and, historically, for people. When the European settlement of North America began more than 500 years ago, in the 1500s, the American shad was found only in the streams and coastal waters of the East Coast. Because shad were so valuable, however, they were introduced in the 1870s into the waters of the West Coast, initially in the Sacramento River of California. Now, they occur in a much larger area along the West Coast of the United States, Canada, and Mexico.

When returning to their home waters to spawn, shad will swim mightily until they reach their birthplace — or until

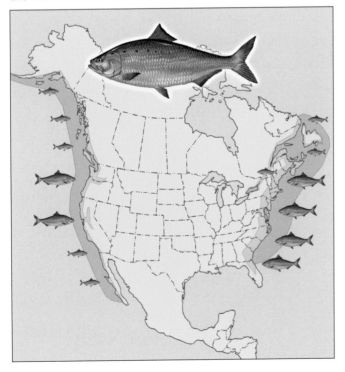

The American shad and its range in the Atlantic and Pacific oceans and adjacent coastal areas of North America. Once found only in the North Atlantic Ocean, the species was introduced into some West Coast rivers and now occurs in the North Pacific Ocean as well.

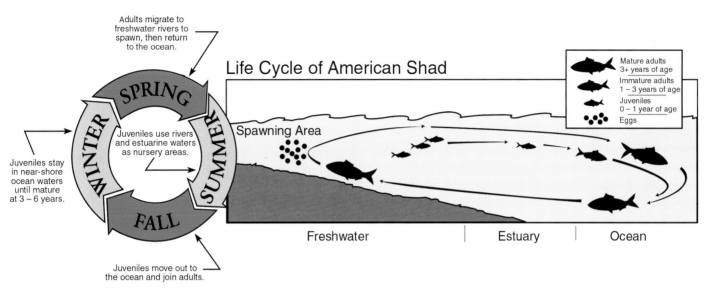

Life Cycle of American Shad

Adults migrate to freshwater rivers to spawn, then return to the ocean.

Juveniles use rivers and estuarine waters as nursery areas.

Juveniles stay in near-shore ocean waters until mature at 3 – 6 years.

Juveniles move out to the ocean and join adults.

Spawning Area

Mature adults
3+ years of age

Immature adults
1 – 3 years of age

Juveniles
0 – 1 year of age

Eggs

Freshwater | Estuary | Ocean

American shad are born in freshwater environments, but they quickly move into an oceanic environment where, for the first few years of their lives, they primarily inhabit near-shore areas. As adults, they move into the open ocean, but in the spring these adults return to the area of their birth to spawn.

they are prevented from doing so by some obstacle, such as a dam. Unlike salmon, shad do not jump, so they cannot get past even very low dams to reach what were formerly spawning grounds.

RIVERS, DAMS, AND FISH: A HISTORICAL RELATIONSHIP

Water falls and natural dams — such as stone ledges, beaver dams, or fallen logs — are normal features of many rivers and smaller streams, and they provide necessary habitat for many aquatic animals such as fish, amphibians, and insects.

Early human inhabitants of North America added their own sometimes-dam-like structures, called weirs, to the streams, lake shores, and coastlines, in order to trap fish to eat. European settlers

This view of Native Americans fishing off the coast of North Carolina or Virginia during the late part of the sixteenth century shows at least three fishweirs in use. Numerous fishweirs, often but not always V-shaped, were used in rivers and smaller streams throughout much of North America.

Little Falls and Little Falls dams on the Potomac River. Shad were once able to swim upstream past Little Falls during their spring migration, but they were not able to cross the higher dams once they were built.

came and began building numerous larger, permanent dams to provide water power to mills for grinding grain, making cloth, or other uses, and to aid navigation through canals. Later, dams were built to create water reservoirs, to supply electricity to cities, or to control runoff and flooding.

In rivers across our continent, dams such as the one at Little Falls, Maryland, blocked the great migrations of anadromous fish and prevented them from reaching their traditional spawning grounds. With less suitable habitat available in which to lay their eggs, combined with the effects of pollution and over harvesting, fish populations such as the Potomac's shad declined significantly.

The Potomac River is a large river with a watershed that drains parts of Maryland, Pennsylvania, Virginia, West Virginia, and Washington, DC, before it

flows into the Chesapeake Bay and then the Atlantic Ocean. The first dam across the Potomac was Little Falls Dam, located ten miles downstream from Great Falls. Little Falls Dam was built in the early 1800s to supply water to the new Chesapeake and Ohio (C&O) Canal that connected Washington, DC, to points west. A second, larger dam was added later at the same location to help provide drinking water to Washington.

Just over ten miles upstream from Little Falls is Great Falls, the natural barrier to the upstream migration of American shad in the Potomac River. Little Falls Dam, however, prevented migrating shad from reaching those ten miles of what had been their traditional spawning grounds.

While the shad were unable to reach their spawning grounds, they were also being heavily harvested. In just over 200 years, the American shad fishery went from being the largest and most valuable

The watershed of the Potomac River includes all of the District of Columbia and parts of four states.

WATERSHED

We all live in a watershed. A *watershed* is the total land area from which water drains into a marsh, stream, river, lake, estuary, or other bodies of water. Watersheds have boundaries: a watershed can be quite large, such as the Chesapeake Bay watershed, or small, such as the watershed of a tiny stream or pond. The Potomac River watershed featured in this book includes more than 14,000 square miles of land. Watersheds can extend across county, state, or national boundaries. Each watershed includes, and is influenced by, everything inside its boundaries — soil, forests, animals, people, farms, highways, industries, and so on. Human activities in watersheds — such as dumping trash into a stream, applying too much fertilizer on a yard, paving large areas of land — can influence the health of both the watershed and the body of water into which it drains.

fishery on the Potomac River to being closed in 1982 because so few shad remained.

In the 1980s, efforts to restore the shad fishery emerged. A government task force proposed a plan to allow the fish to by-pass Little Falls Dam. If a fishway were built into the dam, then the shad could swim through the structure to reach their traditional upstream spawning and nursery areas. The idea of the Little Falls Dam fishway got a boost in 1993 when the federal and state agencies that made up the Chesapeake Bay Program announced a plan to reopen more than 1,347 miles of streams to fish migration and spawning by

modifying or removing dams throughout the Bay's watershed.

In 1995, as part of this large program, biologists led by Jim Cummins from the Interstate Commission on the Potomac River Basin began releasing hatchery-raised American shad above Little Falls Dam. Eggs had been collected from shad caught in the Potomac River, then hatched in the US Fish and Wildlife Service's Harrison Lake National Fish Hatchery. After the young fish were released, they would make their way to the Atlantic Ocean. Later, as adults, they would instinctively try to return to the area where they had been released in order to spawn. Hopefully, the Little Falls Dam fishway would be in place when they returned.

Jim invited Sandi Geddes, a Westbrook Elementary School teacher, and her fifth-grade Aqua Eagles Stream Team to participate in the program. The students would learn how to collect eggs from captured adult shad and how to raise and release their own young fish.

Young American shad make their way down river to the ➡ sea where they will live for several years, then return to the place where they were born to lay eggs and create another generation.

THE NATIONAL FISH PASSAGES PROGRAM

With the Potomac and Susquehanna rivers of the Chesapeake Bay watershed as models, the US Fish and Wildlife Service created the National Fish Passages Program in 1999. This program works with communities, organizations, and agencies to restore waterflow in streams nationwide that will allow fish to once again migrate into waters that were not accessible to them because of dams and other blockages.

The students also would help create awareness within their community of the need for the fishway at Little Falls Dam.

What happened over the next eight years is a unique environmental success that both revitalized the Potomac River and its threatened fish and benefitted the lives of participating students and their communities. Here is their story.

Mount Vernon, George Washington's home in northern Virginia, overlooked the Potomac River. Following in the footsteps of Washington, students who took part in the shad restocking program would tour Mount Vernon and learn that Washington was a fisherman as well as a farmer. When Washington was alive, the students would discover, shad had been caught by nets in the river and brought back to Mount Vernon where they were salted and packed into barrels to be eaten later by farm residents or shipped to far away places such as the West Indies. As part of their tour, the students would board a fishing boat at Mount Vernon's dock and travel to George Washington's traditional fishing grounds on the river. Here, they would help catch adult shad and collect their eggs for use in the shad restocking program.

1995

Great Falls, Maryland: Aqua Eagles Begin the Journey

Nick and Julia scrambled up the steep cliff and looked over the edge. Down below them the swirling waters of the Potomac River sparkled in the sun. Were there fish among the waves? Just above them they could hear the dull roar of Great Falls, a series of large waterfalls that crash down nearly one hundred feet. Other than the American eel, no fish, not even the strong swimming shad, could swim upstream past this rocky barrier.

The two fourth graders had come with their class from Westbrook Elementary School to help biologists with the US

Nick and some of his classmates near the edge of a cliff overlooking Great Falls.

Great Falls is a natural barrier to the upstream movement of shad and most other kinds of fish.

Fish and Wildlife Service release almost one million baby American shad. Below them they could see a large hatchery truck full of the baby fish. In a few moments these tiny shad would be released into the river.

"Let's go, we've got to help them," Julia called to Nick. Cameras clicked at them. They were going to be in the newspaper!

But would the baby shad survive once they let them go? And where would

they go? Nick wondered as he climbed down to the beach.

At the beach Nick and Julia grabbed their buckets of baby shad and headed for the water. Thousands of other baby fish about half an inch long were being pumped into the river from the truck.

"They look like insects," Nick said as he watched the tiny shad darting about in his bucket.

Carefully Nick and Julia lowered their buckets into the river. Even their teacher, Sandi Geddes, put in a bucket of fish. Slowly all of their fish swam out into the flowing water.

Fisheries biologist Jim Cummins cheered them on. "Your young shad have begun a great journey. They will swim from this beach all the way out the Potomac River, through the Chesapeake Bay, and into the Atlantic Ocean to grow up. They are anadromous, and in three to six years, these fish will miraculously return to this very spot to spawn. But," said Jim, "they might hit one big obstacle."

"What could that be?" asked Julia.

"A dam," replied Jim. "In the spring, shad used to swim up past Washington, DC, to this part of the river. Early references of shad migrations described them as a mass of molten silver flowing up the river. Shad were very important fish. Native Americans fished for them with long nets from these very cliffs. Early settlers and birds, such as bald eagles, depended on them for fresh meat each spring. Generations of people flocked to the river to fish for shad."

"But no shad reach Great Falls anymore," he continued. Jim pointed down river. "Almost fifty years ago Little Falls Dam was built above Washington, DC, to bring water to the city. It blocked the fish from returning and laying their eggs in over ten miles of the Potomac River, all the way up to Great Falls. Many people are working to get a notch cut into the dam to create a fishway. That would allow shad to swim through the dam and return here to lay their eggs."

"Your class can help the shad come back," he said to Julia and her fourth grade friends. "You can raise your own shad next year and release them here too."

Julia and Nick were excited. With the help of the Izaak Walton League and their county's Stream Team Program, Westbrook school had formed a stream team named the Aqua Eagles. The club had decided to adopt and help restore Little Falls stream, which flowed right by their school and into the Potomac River at

Little Falls Dam. Cleaning up and restoring their stream *and* raising shad would be great club projects.

"We can really help the river by raising these fish," said Nick.

"Even if we raise and release them," wondered Mrs. Geddes to Jim, "would they survive their great journey? Would the fishway be built in time for their shad to use it to come back to Great Falls?" And, the students wondered, "Would the river run silver again?"

No one knew for sure.

Students and teachers from Westbrook Elementary School assemble along the Potomac River to watch the release of American shad fry into the Potomac River in 1995.

1996

Aqua Eagles Raise and Release the First Generation of Shad

Julia and Nick returned to Westbrook school for their fifth-grade school-year. They joined the Aqua Eagles Stream Team and set out to learn about their adopted stream, Little Falls.

After studying maps, the Aqua Eagles learned that all of the water that ran off their schoolyard flowed to Little Falls stream. This was their school's "Watershed Address." Throughout the fall, all the Aqua Eagles worked hard to help clean up their stream. Each Wednesday, they picked up trash, monitored water quality, or planted trees.

Early in the spring, Chesapeake Bay Foundation Schools in Schools staff came to Westbrook and held a training session on how to raise shad. The Aqua Eagles, together with teachers from three other schools, learned how to set up and run a fish tank and care for shad fry. A grant from Chesapeake Bay Trust paid for materials.

Two large trashcans stacked up within a wooden frame made up the tank. Aqua Eagles hauled buckets of water to fill it. They lowered in pumps and turned them on. Oxygen bubbled

Students at Westbrook school learn how to set up the tank in which their shad will be kept.

into the water. Everyone learned how to test the tank water for oxygen and ammonia and how to raise tiny brine shrimp to feed their baby shad.

Each Aqua Eagle chose a job to do to

care for the tank. Julia chose to bring ice to cool the water. Nick chose to feed the fish. Each student practiced his or her job. By the end of the day the tank was ready. The students couldn't wait to get their fish.

"Now it's time to collect shad eggs," Jim told the Aqua Eagles. "It's time to go fishing and I'll need volunteers to help. We'll fish with Louis Harley, the last full time waterman left in this part of the Potomac River. His family has been fishing for shad for five generations."

"We'll go!" volunteered Nick and classmate Karna. The fishing trip was on.

With great excitement Nick, Karna, Mrs. Geddes, and Jim boarded Louis Harley's fishing boat. They sped out across the Potomac River in the glow of the setting sun. Shad spawn at dusk.

"We have to catch the tide just right," said Louis as he positioned the boat next to a large buoy. "For generations my family has caught shad at this spot. We'd like to see them come back all around the river."

"This is near where George Washington fished for shad," Jim announced to the new fishermen. "We're just downstream from his farm, Mount Vernon. His men set out nets and hauled thousands of shad up onto the beaches. They ate them or salted and shipped them to faraway places. During their awful winter at Valley Forge, George Washington

Fisherman Louis Harley takes the students to catch shad in the Potomac River.

Jim and Mrs. Geddes set the shad net.

Success! Some shad have been caught and Mrs. Geddes is taking one from the net.

saved his troops by feeding them shad from the Delaware and Potomac rivers."

With great expertise, Louis showed Nick and Mrs. Geddes how to lay the net out off the boat and into the water. "Watch the floats on the net. When they sink or bob up and down, we know we've caught fish," he explained.

After a few minutes Mrs. Geddes called out, "They're sinking!" They had caught something. Carefully, they pulled the nets back.

"Here, like this," coached Louis, as Nick and Mrs. Geddes pulled large silvery shad from the nets. "Place them in the live well so that we can take them to the beach and collect their eggs."

Once on the beach with their fish, Nick and the other fishermen squeezed eggs out of the female shad and put them into silver bowls. Next they squeezed the male shad to get their milt. Carefully, they dripped the milt all over the eggs to fertilize them.

Jim and a student squeeze eggs from a female shad into a collecting container.

Gently, they added river water to the bowls, mixing eggs and milt. Within minutes, the eggs swelled to the size of small golden pearls and seemed to glow in the moonlight. Back at Louis's beach, they placed the eggs and water in bags with oxygen.

Jim drove through the night to deliver the fresh eggs to the Harrison Lake National Fish Hatchery, near Richmond, Virginia. There, he met head fisheries biologist Albert Spells and his staff. They placed the pearl-like eggs into hatching jars. Within four days the eggs went from golden pearls to hatching fish.

Back at Westbrook school, all of the students nervously awaited their baby shad. They were ready. A week after the fishing trip, Albert arrived at Westbrook with bags holding their baby shad.

"They look like two eyes and a wiggle," exclaimed Julia, as Albert opened the bags and poured baby shad into the tank.

Students peered into the tank and saw thousands of baby shad swirling about in the water. They swam constantly. Nick squeezed live brine shrimp into the tank. Tiny shad darted about to eat them.

"How will we know that these are our fish?" Mrs. Geddes asked Albert.

"We dipped your baby fish in tetracycline, an antibiotic," he replied. "This marks the young shad's otoliths, some-

BONES IN A SHAD'S HEAD TELL ITS AGE

Shad have several small bones in their skull that are called otoliths. Every day of its life, a fish adds a new ring to each otolith, rings similar to those you can see on a cut tree trunk. Once formed, the rings of an otolith are permanent.

Biologists who raise fish in hatcheries sometimes mark those fish before they are released into the wild. One way to do this is to dip the baby fish into water containing the antibiotic tetracycline. Tetracycline is taken up by the fish, and some of it ends up in the rings of the otoliths that form that day. When an otolith that has been marked with tetracycline is cut and put under an ultraviolet light, the ring that contains tetracycline glows yellow-green in color. Fish that have been marked this way, released into the wild, and later caught and examined can provide biologists and others with important information about the biology and ecology of the fish and the success of the hatchery operation.

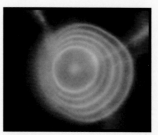

4
mm

An otolith of an adult fish. The actual size of this bone is 4 mm, the length of the short black bar shown above.

The yellow-green glow of the rings in this otolith of a five-day-old shad identifies a fish that was treated with tetracycline.

times called the earbones, with a glowing yellow ring. They'll carry that mark all of their lives."

All the Aqua Eagles helped take care of their shad. They invited each class in the school to visit their tank and gave presentations on their rapidly growing fish. People, including

Aqua Eagles carry a bucket containing young shad to the Potomac River for release.

news reporters, came from all over the Washington area to see the exciting aquaculture project at Westbrook Elementary. After a few weeks of daily care, it was time to release their fish into the river.

The Aqua Eagles packed their shad into buckets and headed to a beach on the Potomac River a short distance below Great Falls. As they set up to release the shad, a crowd gathered. Newspaper reporters and even people from a TV station showed up.

Each Aqua Eagle scooped up wriggling baby shad into a cup. All together the students slowly released them into the water.

The Aqua Eagles make the first release of shad that they had raised in their classroom.

The Aqua Eagles making their presentation to Maryland state senators in Annapolis.

Jim Cummins waved his arm at the river. "From this beach, your shad will travel thousands of miles to and then throughout the ocean in search of food, from the Chesapeake Bay to the Bay of Fundy off Nova Scotia. When they reach three to six years old, shad that survive this great journey will return here to the Potomac," he told the Aqua Eagles.

"They'll face many obstacles before they can return," joined Mrs. Geddes. "Can you name a few?"

"Largemouth bass and other fish," exclaimed Nick.

"Birds like bald eagles," added Julia. "And then finally the dam."

But deep in their hearts they knew their shad would return.

After the release, Mrs. Geddes and the Aqua Eagles described their shad project in a presentation at Watershed '96, a national conference of watershed biologists. There they met officials working on removing the dams all around the Chesapeake Bay. They made their case to remove the Little Falls Dam and won a prize for one of the best presentations.

From there they presented their project to legislators in Annapolis, the state capital of Maryland. The Aqua Eagles told of their shad project and about the importance of putting a notch with a fishway into the Little Falls Dam. Their fish would need it to return home. They left the state senators with the mission of helping to get the fishway in place soon, to "Let the river run silver again!"

1999

New Trees and a Rain Garden Help Restore the Watershed

Each year since 1996, a new Aqua Eagles Stream Team had done everything it could to bring the American shad back to that stretch of the Potomac River between Little Falls Dam and Great Falls. Students had written countless letters to politicians to encourage them to build the Little Falls fishway. Aqua Eagles had successfully raised and released four generations of American shad into the Potomac River. With Westbrook school as a model, over twenty schools in the area were now raising shad!

The 1999 Aqua Eagles found that they had an important new mission: to help replant vegetation along the banks of Little Falls stream. A great flood had

> ### STREAMSIDE FORESTS ARE IMPORTANT FOR FISH
>
> The land bordering streams is called the *riparian* zone. Riparian forests and wetlands filter nutrients and sediment, capture rainfall, regulate the flow of water into streams, moderate stream and air temperature, stabilize banks, and create and maintain habitat for both terrestrial and aquatic life. An important tool for restoring the quality of a stream's habitat is to plant trees and establish wetlands on riparian land.

swept through the year before, tearing out trees and wetlands in its path. The Potomac Conservancy had received a grant to repair the damage and invited schools, including Westbrook and its community, to help. The first step was to map the flood damage.

On a rainy September day, Mrs. Geddes led the Aqua Eagles down to Little Falls. Ben Symons, one of the club leaders, helped lead the way.

Bare patches of rain-soaked earth formed muddy streams that flowed beneath the Aqua Eagle's feet and into Little Falls.

"We've got to help stop this mud," said Ben to the club. "The sediment from Little Falls watershed will travel to the

When the shadbush blooms in the spring, it is time for the American shad to return to the rivers of the Chesapeake Bay watershed.

Aqua Eagles plant a shadbush alongside Little Falls stream.

On their first planting day, Aqua Eagles joined foresters, neighbors, and students from other schools. They planted hundreds of different trees, including the very special shadbush.

Matt Berres of the Potomac Conservancy held up a shadbush for all to see.

"Each spring this bush will bloom starry white flowers, heralding the return of the shad to the Potomac River," he explained. " And with the help of these trees, your shad will return to a cleaner river."

Later in the fall, the Aqua Eagles built a rain garden next to their school to help reduce runoff to their stream even more. They built this garden by planting bright red cardinal flowers, sedges, and other wetland plants in a small walled area at the base of the downspout of a rain gutter. Their new rain garden would absorb rainwater that flowed from their school's roof, filtering the water slowly so it could flow clearly into their stream.

Westbrook students prepare a new rain garden.

Potomac River and clog our shads' gills when we release them in the spring. Let's plant trees to help stop it."

State foresters and biologists met with the Aqua Eagles to develop a tree-planting plan for Little Falls. New trees would stabilize the soil. Less soil runoff would clean the stream and help clean the river of sediment. More shade would help cool both Little Falls stream and the Potomac River where the shad spawned each spring.

WETLANDS

Wetlands are poorly drained lands where water strongly influences the types of soils, plants, and animals that occur in the area. A wetland must have a period of time during each year that water is present, have plants adapted to wet soil, and have soils that are low or absent in oxygen due to their saturation in water. There are many types of wetlands, including marshes, bogs, fens, swamps, prairie potholes, and bottomland hardwood forests. Wetlands may not always appear to be wet. Many dry out for extended periods of time. Others may appear dry on the surface but are saturated underneath. Wetlands perform important ecological functions, such as slowing the runoff of water and filtering pollutants from runoff.

In the spring, the Izaak Walton League invited the Aqua Eagles to help restore a natural wetland at their shad release site. The restored wetland would once again serve as a filter for runoff from the flood-damaged land. Park rangers joined the students and Izaak Walton League volunteers to turn a muddy hole into a young wetland filled with cardinal flowers and shadbushes.

At their shad release in May, the Aqua Eagles were pleased to see their shadbushes in bloom. But would these blooms ever signal the return of shad to Great Falls?

◆ A cardinalflower plant blooms in the new wetland.

2000

The Fishway Goes In and the Shad Return!

Each year after the first shad release, Mrs. Geddes' new Aqua Eagles class traveled by boat to catch shad and collect their eggs on the river with Jim Cummins and Louis Harley. And each spring the Aqua Eagles raised hundreds of baby shad in their school tanks and released them above the Little Falls Dam at Great Falls.

Finally, in January of 2000, the US Army Corps of Engineers completed the Little Falls Dam fishway. All of the letters that the Aqua Eagles had written since 1995, together with their presentations at the Watershed '96 conference and to the legislators, had been a big help in getting the job done. Mrs. Geddes and the Aqua Eagles were invited to the opening of the new fishway to be recognized for their important work!

On May 22, 1995, the *Washington Post* published the diagrams at right to show the location and shape of the Little Falls fishway. This structure, called a labyrinth weir fishway, consists of a notch placed in the upper edge of the dam and a series of W-shaped weirs that slow the flowing water and allow the fish to swim up to and through the notch. The photograph below shows the nearly finished fishway under construction.

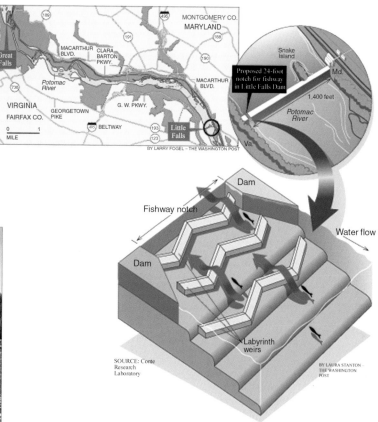

Ben Symons, student at Westbrook school, taking part in the ceremony opening the Little Falls fishway in 1999. Pictured here are Congresswoman Connie Morella; Mufeed Odeh, US Geological Survey, designer of the fishway; Ben Symons; Senator Paul Sarbanes; and Secretary of the Interior Bruce Babbit.

Aqua Eagle member Ben Symons stood at the edge of the new fishway with Secretary of the Interior Bruce Babbitt, US Senator Paul Sarbanes, and other dignitaries.

Ben gave a speech in which he said, "When I was in first grade, some Aqua Eagles made a speech over the PA system. This was the first time I heard about the fish called shad. Last year, when I was in

Spawning American shad swirl in the water below a dam.

fourth grade, I got to make the hatchery for the brine shrimp that were used to feed the shad. This year, Aqua Eagles will fish for shad, do presentations, and train teachers who are new to shad. I'm glad that the notch is finally made in Little Falls Dam so that all the Westbrook shad will have the opportunity to get back home to reproduce."

In April, divers filmed thousands of river herring moving up Little Falls towards the dam. Behind river herring would come the shad. The fishway was ready. But would it work?

THE SHAD RETURN

Excitement filled the air as Ben and the Aqua Eagles released their tiny shad fry below Great Falls later that spring. Had the shad that had been released years ago returned? Students peered carefully into the water to see if there were adult shad among the river grass, but saw none.

Farther upstream, Jim Cummins, and Mike Odom, biologist with the US Fish and Wildlife Service, prepared to try to catch some shad. Just as Native Americans and European colonists had done years before, they were going to capture shad using a dip net — a circular net on a long pole.

Attempts to catch fish with other nets had failed. The rocks were too numerous; boats could not fit among them. Even canoe fishing was dangerous.

Jim Cummins preparing to net shad in the Potomac River.

Standing on a steep cliff, Jim dunked the dip net into the river, felt a pull, and there it was — a shad! Mike then netted two more. The shad had made it over the dam and returned to Great Falls.

Carefully, the fish were saved and sent to the Virginia Institute of Marine Science. There, fisheries biologists tested the fish's otoliths. One of them turned out to have the hatchery mark made by the tetracycline. The released shad had returned, after five years!

Other shad were caught down river. Many had the mark. They were not yet above the Little Falls Dam, but they were on their way.

An artist's impression of shad emerging from the labyrinth weir fishway at Little Falls Dam.

2003

Aqua Eagles Reunite for Seventh-Generation Shad

Julia rowed her crew boat up the Potomac River. She was now a senior at Walt Whitman High School and on the rowing team. Each time she rowed across the waters of the river, she'd look for fish under her boat. It was early spring and, although the water was still cold, she could see thousands of fish passing under the boat. Were some of them their shad? She'd heard last spring that some shad had been netted at Great Falls. Was the fishway working?

Julia had become vice president of her high school ecology club. She had continued her interest in science after raising shad and now wanted to do a real life science project.

Julia chose to raise river grass to plant in the river. Her club set up large shallow tanks to raise river grasses such as wild celery. The club members planted the grasses in the Potomac River near Mount Vernon. More grasses would provide food and shelter for fish such as the shad she had released years ago.

Nick was also a senior in high school. Inspired in part by his work with the shad project, he chose to focus on chemistry.

Julia, in the center and now in high school, rowing across the Potomac.

He had just been awarded a full scholarship in chemical engineering by Tulane University. For fun, he hiked and fished around Great Falls. Each time he fished he wondered about the shad. Were they coming back? Would he catch one?

In February, Mrs. Geddes met with Schools in Schools staff to prepare to raise her seventh generation of shad. Jim Cummins came to give an update on the shad project.

"We captured twelve shad at Great Falls last year, and four of them had our mark!" he exclaimed to the excited teachers. "The fishway is working. Our shad have returned to Great Falls! We've also seen more shad in the river this year than ever before."

Back at school, Mrs. Geddes couldn't wait to tell her students the news. "The shad have come back," she announced. "Some of them have our mark! Now we know that we're really making a difference." Her class cheered.

Julia's brother Eli was one of Mrs. Geddes' fourth grade students. He was going to help raise shad and knew that Julia had helped raise those first fish. Mrs. Geddes let Julia, Nick, and other first generation shad parents know that their fish had returned.

When Julia got the news she was thrilled. She wanted to come celebrate the return of the shad with Mrs. Geddes and the Aqua Eagles.

Back in her old classroom, Julia was amazed at how the project had changed. Students were now hatching their shad eggs and raising the baby fish too. Living Classrooms Foundation had joined the project and gotten special chillers donated for the tanks. Chillers kept the tank water cold like the river's water.

A large TV screen showed the pearl-like eggs. Shad embryos wiggled inside

Like tiny pearls, shad eggs lie in a container beneath the watchful eye of a camera before hatching.

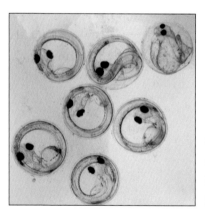

Shad embryos as they continue to develop in their egg cases.

Shad eggs showing the development of embryos just before hatching.

A newly hatched shad larva with egg sac still present. ➡

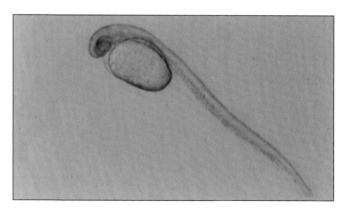

the egg cases. Some hatched and swam about with yolk sacs still attached. Fifth graders made a presentation on their shad project to the third grade, and Julia was their special guest.

"This project just gets better and better," Julia announced to the fourth-grade class as she surveyed their shad tank. "We calculated that we'd be in high school when our shad returned, and they have," she continued. "Now with the fishway in, your fish will be able to come back to Great Falls too." The class ap-

plauded excitedly. They couldn't wait to release their baby shad.

Mrs. Geddes brought out a special treat. She had fished for shad the night before and smoked some for everyone to try. It was cooked just as George Washington would have done. "The Latin name for shad is *Alosa sapidissima*, meaning most delicious herring," she explained. Julia and the class agreed. It was delicious.

This year's Aqua Eagles led Julia on a tour of Westbrook's new restoration

Julia and Nick return to take part in the release of shad fry by Westbrook students in 2003.

projects. Trays of green wild celery grass bound for the Potomac River bubbled in the classroom. Westbrook's fish program had expanded to raising rainbow trout that would be released into Seneca Creek, a stream that flows into the Potomac River just above Great Falls. A large 100-gallon tank stood across from the shad tank, filled with colorful jumping baby trout.

In a week it was time to release the seventh generation of baby shad. On the day of the release, Julia joined the class. Word of the return of the fish had spread, and Nick had gotten the news. He also joined to help with the release and to meet the new Aqua Eagles.

Students hauled the heavy buckets of baby shad and water down to the river, with Julia and Nick by their sides. At the river's edge they unfurled their "Goodbye Shad" sign. Julia and Nick stood before the class with Mrs. Geddes.

"When we released our baby shad," Julia said to the group, "we knew it would be a long, perilous journey for them. They'd have to travel all the way to the Atlantic Ocean and then back here to lay their eggs."

"We somehow knew they'd make it up the fishway if it was built," added Nick. "Our prediction was correct."

Biologist Jim stood next to Julia and Nick and pointed upstream towards the roar of Great Falls.

"We caught a marked fish at the base of Great Falls!" he exclaimed to the crowd gathered at the river's edge. "For the first time in almost sixty years shad are back to Great Falls. Other marked fish have been caught just downstream of the dam. We've seen more shad in the river this year than we've ever seen before."

Just then an osprey circled above them. "Birds such as that osprey and even bald eagles will benefit from the shad coming back," Mrs. Geddes explained, "as well as all the other creatures of the river, including us."

Mrs. Geddes, the Aqua Eagles, and many proud parents scooped up cups of wriggling baby shad out of their buckets. Cameras clicked. Onlookers cheered. Carefully the students released their tiny shad into the river to start their own great journey, with Julia and Nick cheering them on.

For yet another time, the students of Westbrook say "Goodbye" to their shad, and wish them well on their long journey to the ocean.

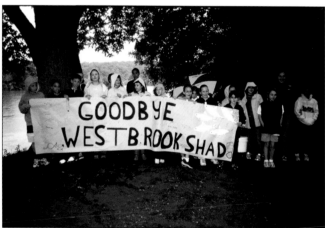

Epilogue

Generations of Westbrook students have been, and will continue to be, inspired by the knowledge, awareness, and accomplishments that resulted from their participation in the shad project. Likewise, the Potomac River and its watershed have benefitted from the students' efforts to restore and maintain the area's environmental health.

Teacher Sandi Geddes and her fourth-grade students and fifth-grade Aqua Eagles Stream Team, together with students and teachers at more than forty other schools in the Washington, DC, area, are still raising shad and bay grasses, planting native trees, maintaining rain gardens, and in other ways perpetuating the tradition of environmental stewardship established by the shad project.

Westbrook Elementary School has been honored by the State of Maryland for its comprehensive environmental program by being named a Green School.

Westbrook students Julia and Nick credit their experience with the shad restoration project for helping inspire them to pursue careers in science, Julia at Cornell University and Nick at Tulane University.

Shad program students such as Tom Gray are using their skills in stream conservation to help other river commu-

Over the years, many students in the Washington, DC, area raised young shad and released them into the Potomac River. How, they wondered, would their efforts improve the health of the shad population and the Chesapeake Bay ecosystem?

nities. Tom sent information on the Potomac shad project to the Mattaponi Indian Reservation to help them make a case for preserving their historical shad spawning grounds in Virginia's Mattaponi River.

Several former Aqua Eagles have either published papers or been the subject of publications. In 1997, while still in middle school, Michael Robinson and Trevor Swett published a short paper in *Shad Journal* titled "The shad project: Students strive to restore shad in the Potomac using a full shad system." Ben Symons, who spoke at the opening of the Little Falls Dam fishway, is featured in one chapter in the book *Saving the Bay: People Working for the Future of the Chesapeake,* published in 2001 by Johns Hopkins University Press.

All students who participated in the shad project contributed to the success of the effort and can legitimately be proud of having helped rehabilitate the important shad populations in the historic Potomac River.

SCHOOLS AND BIOLOGISTS: PARTNERS IN SUCCESS

From 1995 to 2002, biologists stocked over sixteen million American shad in the Potomac River. Some of these young fish would return as adults and migrate upstream through Little Falls Dam, once the fish passage was installed.

Chief Lone Eagle Custalow of the Mattaponi Indian Reservation holds a shad.

School participation in the project grew from the involvement of Westbrook and three other schools in 1995 to include over forty schools and thousands of students in the Washington, DC, area.

Beginning in 1995, students released over 150,000 American shad fry into the Potomac River. To provide a healthier environment to which their fish could return, the shad schools worked hard planting countless trees and created or revitalized wetlands and rain gardens throughout the Potomac River watershed.

Over the next eight years, river grasses increased in the Potomac River and the water quality improved. Little Falls Dam got its fishway and, in the end, all who participated in the project were able to celebrate the return of the threatened American shad to their traditional spawning grounds on that part of the Potomac River below Great Falls.

As of 2004, the number of adult American shad netted for egg collection had more than doubled since the stocking program began, and the number of young shad captured was almost eight times the record that existed prior to the completion of the Little Falls fish passage project.

VISIT GREAT FALLS AND SEE THE RETURNING SHAD

Great Falls is bordered by two national parks, the Chesapeake & Ohio Canal National Historical Park in Maryland and Great Falls Park of the George Washington Memorial Parkway in Virginia. A spectacular view of the falls awaits visitors at both parks. Should you visit the falls in April, you might even catch a silvery glimpse of returning shad in the swirling waters at the base of the falls.

The students actually released their shad at Angler's Inn, Maryland, almost one mile downstream from Great Falls. Information on the C&O canal park is

The number of shad caught in the Potomac River has increased significantly since the stocking program began in 1995. This chart was prepared by the Interstate Commission on the Potomac River Basin and shows data that were collected by the Maryland Department of Natural Resources as part of that agency's haul seine survey of young-of-the-year shad.

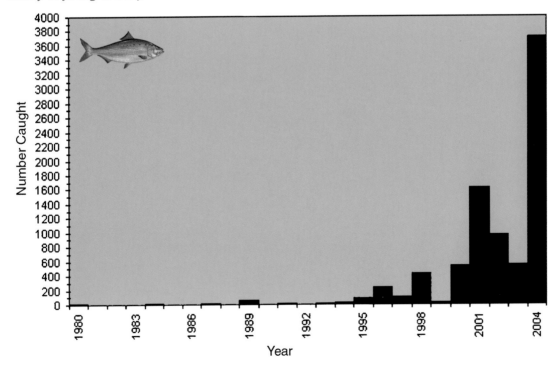

High school students check water quality with National Park Service Ranger Rod Sauter at the Chesapeake & Ohio Canal National Historical Park. These students are participating in the Bridging the Watershed program, a partnership between the Alice Ferguson Foundation and the National Park Service to help students develop a sense of stewardship for natural resources and public lands. For more information, please visit *www.bridgingthewatershed.org.*

available at (301) 299-3613 or from its web site at *www.nps.gov/choh.* Information can be obtained for the Great Falls Park Visitors Center at (703) 285-2763 or from its web site at *www.nps.gov/gwmp/grfa.*

HELPING STUDENTS HELP THE SHAD

The student shad-stocking project in the Potomac River was made possible by a partnership among schools throughout the metropolitan Washington, DC, area and the following conservation organizations and commissions:

Anacostia Watershed Society
www.anacostiaws.org

Chesapeake Bay Foundation
www.cbf.org

Interstate Commission on the Potomac River Basin
www.potomacriver.org

Izaak Walton League of America
www.iwla.org

Living Classrooms
www.livingclassrooms.org

The Potomac Conservancy
www.potomac.org

Glossary

Anadromous fish: Fish that are born in freshwater, migrate to and spend most of their lives in the ocean, and come back to freshwater to spawn. Some species of anadromous fish return to the ocean after they spawn, whereas others die in the freshwater after spawning.

Brine shrimp: Tiny shrimp-like organisms that live in saltwater. Brine shrimp are often raised to feed fish fry.

Ecosystem: A community of animals, plants, and simpler organisms that interact with each other and their physical and chemical environment. An ecosystem can be as small as a puddle, as large as a watershed, or even as large as Earth itself.

Embryo: An organism in the early stages of development, especially before it is hatched or born.

Aqua Eagle Nick is feeding brine shrimp to shad fry in his school's aquaculture tank.

Fertilize: To combine sperm and an egg as the first step in creating new life.

Fishway: A structure that helps fish to pass over, around, or through an obstruction in a waterway.

Fry: Newly hatched baby fish that have used up their yolk sacs and are ready to find their own food.

Larvae: Fish that have just hatched.

Milt: Sperm-filled fluid sprayed onto eggs by a male fish to fertilize the eggs.

Otoliths: Small, paired bones in sacs of the fish's skull used for balance and to detect sounds.

Spawn: The eggs produced by a female fish.

Sperm: The seed of life produced by a male.

Yolk sac: The food supply that is attached to newly hatched fish.

Watershed: The land area from which water drains into a particular stream or lake.

Wetland: A vegetated, poorly drained ecosystem that supports standing water or has very wet soils for some part of the year.

The ultimate success of the shad restocking program, of course, is measured by the presence of shad populations in ever-increasing numbers where, only a few years ago, there had been few or none. ➡

Reflections and Considerations

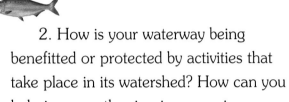

1. Why is a healthy waterway important to you and your community?

2. How is your waterway being benefitted or protected by activities that take place in its watershed? How can you help improve the riparian areas in your watershed?

3. How is your waterway being harmed by activities that take place in its watershed? What can be done to stop or minimize these activities?

4. How is your waterway and its watershed different than it was 500 years ago, when the European colonization of North America began?

5. Why has your waterway and its watershed changed during the past 500 years? When did most of the change take place? How is it still changing?

6. Were there kinds of animals in your waterway long ago that are not present today? If so, why are they not present today? Does suitable habitat exist for these kinds of animals today, or does it need to be restored? Could these animals be reintroduced and, if so, by what agency?

7. Are there any people or groups who are working to improve the health of your waterway or its watershed? Do they need your help?

8. Does the media in your area cover activities that harm or benefit the environmental quality of your watershed and its waters? If yes, how well is it doing? If not, why not – and how can you help to change this?

Seven Steps to a Successful Water, Wetland, or Watershed Project

Opportunities abound for individuals, small groups, and networks of concerned citizens everywhere to become involved in environmental rehabilitation. Here is a short list of some essential steps you can take to learn more about the environmental challenges that exist in your local waterways and watersheds and ways to deal with those challenges.

1. Learn your "watershed address" — the watershed in which you live, work, or play. To find your watershed address, visit the Environmental Protection Agency's Surf Your Watershed page at *www.epa.gov/surf.*

2. Learn more about your watershed. Visit the Watershed Information Network *www.epa.gov/win* to get up-to-date information on your watershed. Buy a topographic map that includes your watershed and outline its boundaries. Learn about the environmental history of your watershed — how has your watershed changed during the past century and what influence did these changes have on the air, land, and water?

3. Explore your waterway and watershed by map, foot, automobile, or boat. Learn to recognize activities that are beneficial or detrimental to the environmental health of your waterway or watershed.

4. Think of or learn about projects that could improve the environmental health of your waterway or watershed. Some projects in which you could take part might already be underway in your watershed. Many resources are identified below from which information about environmental needs or existing projects is available.

5. Select a project. Decide what problems or concerns you want to address, then join an existing group or start an activity of your own, either alone or with the assistance of others.

6. Get funding! Most successful waterway or watershed conservation programs will require funding. There are many potential sources for funding, both governmental and private. Federal agencies that provide funding include the National Oceanic and Atmospheric Administration (*www.noaa.gov*) and the Environmental Protection Agency (*www.epa.gov*). Private sources include Fish America Foundation (*www.fishamerica.org*), the National Fish and Wildlife Foundation (*www.nfwf.org*), and American Rivers (*www.americanrivers.org*).

7. Share the project with your community by involving other people who share your interest in and commitment to environmental health. Make the media aware of your good work and civic responsibility.

SAMPLE PROJECTS

1. Plant native plants — to minimize erosion caused by runoff and provide food and shelter for wildlife.

2. Build a rain garden or wetland to reduce runoff and improve water quality.

3. Plan a trash pickup to improve a stream's appearance as well as to reduce pathogens, toxins, and trash which may harm wildlife.

4. Monitor water quality of your local stream or river – changes in water quality or numbers of aquatic animals can alert you to emerging threats to your stream or river.

5. Help to stock shad, trout, or other fish. Contact your local state fish and game commission or department of natural resources about the schedule of local stocking programs. Not only can you provide labor, but your participation might attract media and community attention that will spotlight the need for stocking programs.

6. Participate in the raising and release of fish by joining programs such as those offered by Trout Unlimited (Trout in the Classroom program) or Sea Grant (coastal states — contact your state university Sea Grant office). Reintroducing fish can help increase populations of fish that have been depleted.

7. Work with local, state or federal politicians and the media on conservation issues that are important to you and your community. Write letters. You and your community's input can make the critical difference in getting something done. Westbrook Elementary was credited as being a catalyst for getting the fishway put into Little Falls Dam in good time.

RESOURCES

Abundant resources exist from which individuals or groups can obtain information about important environmental issues and recommendations for how to deal with them. Below is a list of representative conservation organizations and governmental agencies that can provide information about water, wetland, and watershed rehabilitation programs.

Government Agencies

Chesapeake Bay Program
www.chesapeakebay.net

National Oceanic and Atmospheric Administration
National Sea Grant College Program
www.nsgo.seagrant.org/colleges/ colleges.html

NOAA Fisheries
www.nmfs.noaa.gov

Office of Education
www.education.noaa.gov
www.oesd.noaa.gov

National Park Service
www.nps.gov

US Department of Agriculture
Natural Resources Conservation Service
www.nrcs.usda.gov/feature/backyard

US Environmental Protection Agency
www.epa.gov

Watershed Information Network
www.epa.gov/win

Surf Your Watershed
www.epa.gov/surf

Adopt Your Watershed
www.epa.gov/adopt

Water Resource Center
www.epa.gov/safewater/resource

US Fish and Wildlife Service
www.fws.gov

Some agencies that exist in all states, and typically have offices in many if not all counties, include the following. The names might differ slightly from state to state.

Cooperative Extension Service
Department of Agriculture
Department of Environmental Quality
Department of Health
Department of Natural Resources
River Commission
Soil and Water Conservation District
Wastewater Department

Conservation and Environmental Education Organizations

The following organizations provide educational information about water, watersheds, wetlands, and waterways. Many of these organizations teach people how to work with volunteers to restore watersheds and their habitats, and they provide information on how to form groups to clean up streams and shorelines, monitor water quality, and plant native trees and other plants to help restore waterways, wetlands, or watersheds.

 Adopt-A-Stream Foundation
www.streamkeeper.org

 American Rivers
www.americanrivers.org

 Center for Watershed Protection
www.cwp.org

 Earth Force
Global Rivers Environmental Education Network
www.earthforce.org

 Izaak Walton League of America
Save Our Streams Program
www.iwla.org

 National Wildlife Federation
www.nwf.org

 Ocean Conservancy
www.cmc-ocean.org

 Project Aquatic WILD
Council for Environmental Education
www.projectwild.org

 Project WET
www.projectwet.org

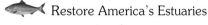 Restore America's Estuaries
www.estuaries.org

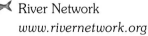 River Network
www.rivernetwork.org

 River of Words
www.riverofwords.org

 Waterkeeper Alliance
www.waterkeeper.org

National organizations that preserve or protect natural habitats include:

 National Audubon Society
www.audubon.org

 The Nature Conservancy
www.tnc.org

 Sierra Club
www.sierraclub.org

Groups that promote specifically fish research and fish habitat conservation, and direct citizen action to help restore and preserve fish populations, include:

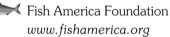 American Fisheries Society
www.fisheries.org

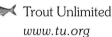 Coastal Conservation Association
www.joinCCA.org

Fish America Foundation
www.fishamerica.org

Trout Unlimited
www.tu.org

Organizations that promote and assist in the planting of native plants include:

Environmental Concern
www.wetland.org

State native plant societies, usually accessible by web search or by visiting
www.acorn-online.com/hedge/h-socs.htm